HOUSE
OF SUGAR,
HOUSE
OF STONE

The Mountain West Poetry Series
Stephanie G'Schwind & Donald Revell, series editors

We Are Starved, by Joshua Kryah
The City She Was, by Carmen Giménez Smith
Upper Level Disturbances, by Kevin Goodan
The Two Standards, by Heather Winterer
Blue Heron, by Elizabeth Robinson
Hungry Moon, by Henrietta Goodman
The Logan Notebooks, by Rebecca Lindenberg
Songs, by Derek Henderson
The Verging Cities, by Natalie Scenters-Zapico
A Lamp Brighter than Foxfire, by Andrew S. Nicholson
House of Sugar, House of Stone, by Emily Pérez

HOUSE
OF SUGAR,
HOUSE
OF STONE

POEMS

EMILY PÉREZ

The Center for Literary Publishing
Colorado State University

For information about permission to reproduce
selections from this book, write to
The Center for Literary Publishing
attn: Permissions
9105 Campus Delivery, Colorado State University
Fort Collins, Colorado 80523-9105.

Printed in the United States of America.

Library of Congress Cataloging-in-Publication Data

Names: Pérez, Emily (Poet), author.
Title: House of sugar, house of stone : poems / Emily Pérez.
Description: Fort Collins : The Center for Literary Publishing, Colorado
    State University, [2016] | Series: The mountain west poetry series | These
    poems are suggested by themes and characters found in Grimms' Fairy Tales.
    | Description based on print version record and CIP data provided by
    publisher; resource not viewed.
Identifiers: LCCN 2015049833 (print) | LCCN 2015048598 (ebook) | ISBN
    9781885635501 (electronic) | ISBN 9781885635495 | ISBN
    9781885635495 (pbk. : alk. paper)
Subjects: LCSH: Kinder- und Hausmärchen--Poetry. | Fairy tales--Poetry.
Classification: LCC PS3616.E74327 (print) | LCC PS3616.E74327 H68 2016
    (ebook) | DDC 811/.6--dc23
LC record available at http://lccn.loc.gov/2015049833

The paper used in this book meets the minimum requirements of the American National
Standard for Information Sciences-Permanence of Paper for Printed Library Materials,
ANSI Z39.48-1984.

1 2 3 4 5   20 19 18 17 16

For Wylan, Felix, and Matt—into the woods and out again.

The children must go,
we will take them farther into the wood,
so that they will not find their way out again;
there is no other means of saving ourselves!

—The Brothers Grimm, "Hansel and Gretel"

CONTENTS

I.

II.

I.

LULLABY

Where is the girl who hid in the woods

when wolves came.   Where is the boy

who broke brambles with his hands.

        Why were the two setting down stones

and where should the stones have pointed.

Which were the minutes they felt most alone:

        before the wind wept   or after, once sure

of what awaited.   What words did they slip

to the shivering air   and what was the sound

                that silenced. What did the owl's eye   blink from

that night   when the moon refused   to linger.

        Where did the mouse spill his hard-won crumb

when the shadow passed slow over.

        Did the tree's hollow not hold?
        Was the river too wild to ford?
        Why so still, why so still, and why no fire

yet burning.   *Who* mouths the mouse.
                How moans the owl.
                And *when* cries the on-blowing wind.

3

UNDER THE ROOF

Under the roof, the shingled roof, no,
    under the eaves, the leaf-clawed eaves,
no, under the clouds collecting slow
    sloughing glass, glitter missives now
under the evergreens that grow
    over the snow where wolf feet go
feather-light, nails tap-ticking,
    frost clicking as pine needles ever
fall and flow, those slivered, silvered
    spines of sap, sweet poison-tipped,
designed to stick, like silent wishes slipped
    under the snow by one who waits
under the eye, the eye divine measuring
    each gasp and murmur, the weight
of days, the whims of weather, the webs
    of lovers, spells of spiders, throes, thralls,
trembling of each quarry's cover
    under the reach of the past and closer
under the gaze that hovers cold
    over the scene like a broad-winged hawk,
the gaze that knows what never was,
    what never shall be, what lies shut,
    what's still
beneath each breath and shudder.

EACH DAY I OPEN THE DOOR TO DAMAGE

I dust, and the lampshade's glass
                    erupts
        to shards that scar the floor

        I scour my car, sponge brutish
                        cursive across its hull

                                While tending the dogs
                I let my laptop drown
                        on a chair on the deck, a day rain-full—
                                corrosion sprouts like eerie moss,
                                turquoise, winking from each crevasse

I'm armed and killing with my care

        Now you, still forming—your pink cup ears
                just nerve-lined enough
                to hear my voice, unbidden—
                                Your skin's membrane
                                        constant sieving
                                        wine, caffeine,
        hormones I down for our bound health—
                                Even the peroxide I pour
                                to scrub the bath, protecting
                                us from moldy blooms—

        moods, fears, shuddering doubt

So much your doorways can't keep out

My cells storm your little rooms

DIRECTIONS

The toothy man shows me.
The toothy man knows. Fingers
my basket, my meats, my rolls,
my treats and sweet deliverables,
sniffs at my clothes, pulls
at my hem of worsted wool
with cared-for nails, carefully
he lays out the way: a line in the loam,
a stack of white stones
on featherbed moss, transcribes
a map of missteps, misthoughts.

A NEW MOTHER DISCOVERS EMPTINESS

That winter I resigned my role as hope—
with only two hands, smaller always than I'd needed,
and twice as many yearning mouths to fill.
I concocted stories, songs, and spells,
and once we'd sucked the marrow clean
from words, I spun, I wove, I kept conniving to confect,
but there's only so much sweetness in the world.
I poured pity on the two of them,
just children still, all their pleasure flown.
In each other's faces we reflected want,
so I sought solace on my own.
I found it first within the darkness of the woods,
which rendered me invisible. I found it next
within the distance of the stars, whispering how miniscule,
how meaningless my sorrows. Who insists on being heard
when faced with all that space? What is emptiness
when perched upon the lip of a black hole?
I tried to teach those little ones to see,
I pushed them toward the door.
And when they would not go, I locked them out myself.
Here is a pathway, here is bread, I said, *you'll learn
these walls were never real. Make a new home
inside your head.* To those who ask me,
What if they are calling in the woods?
I say, *at least they've learned to sing*
and to those who wonder *what if
they're trembling with fear?*
I say, *then at last they're full.*

SELF PORTRAIT AS A DAM

Sweet-seeded like a watermelon
And just as juice infused

Or did I harbor swamps in me
Veiled vapors layered

    Reservoir, retaining.

Pass me through a pastry press
To thin this risen dough

Set me on a desert rock
To sizzle like a lizard

Or better, poke straws
In all my pores and suck

    Plump pocket, undraining.

I see the sense in leeches
I see the need for laboring

In oasisless space under unrelenting
Heat lamps, foil-bound

Swathed in sweaters, rolled in
Unbreathable leather like a wrestler

    Before weigh in, praying.

Big ship on land
No small sea will carry me

The Dutch boy must die
Or thumb some other problem

Once the plug is fled
I'll flood and slough and sieve

    Sodden husk, remaining.

THE FLOOD

Early in her stay, Grandmother
teaches me the word "abscond."
A portion of her sandwich hits the floor

where the cat, that selfish hunter, mouths it quickly,
"absconding with the turkey."
Outdoors, I show her the mass migration of ants.

A day's irrigation floods their homes,
and we wade ankle-deep, indifferent to the deluge.
Hordes raft to safety on stray branches, transmit

silent signals to those beyond the water's lip
who scrabble further afield to beat disaster
heads laden with leaves, eggs, what they've salvaged

of their nest's essential infrastructure.
My grandmother lets slip an *oh!*
of delight, she may even clap her tiny hands.

Before her, this family: a finely tuned machine,
working in concert toward survival, struggling
to save its queen.

MOTHER LOVE

The wave that surges when I watch the childless penguins chase the hatchling, caught and drifting from his nest (ten females packed in rugby scrum, baby as ball) is not a wave of shock, but recognition. Each hen cranes to get her beak upon his down-ruffed neck, to prove herself the best at mothering, a show of force and pecking.

And when the prim-accented nature-show narrator says, "often, the chick does not survive the fray" (the camera cuts away, discreet, to pan along the icy ground), I know that in my life the camera keeps on rolling, leaving a de-feathered thing, held close too long, in focus, limp and quivering.

THE MEOW'S THE THING—

that plaintive gate-
way into want, an
inter- intra- species
siren yawning
toward the fire.

I once danced with
a man, a stranger
who let his meow
fly, like a vast helium
balloon he didn't know

he held, and watched
float off in mixed-
up awe and sorrow.
I bowed to this
unbridled yowl,

then fled.

FURTHER THOUGHTS ON RESPONSIBILITY

Dear H, the priest says forgive. I try.
To see things in her way, second wife,
sequestered in a woodsman's dusty home.
Two silent kids, their games with stones,
a husband mired in aloneness. Remember
Papa whittling through the night: bears
and spoons, pinecones, and birds. And then
he carved the means to get away: the rough canoe,
the walking stick. We didn't blame. We all longed
for anywhere. He went from woodworking to wandering,
past the farthest cuckoo's cry, and he'd return
in three days' time, hollow cheeked, hollow eyed,
and us too small to heft an axe or haul real wood.
As if he thought one day we'd walk in from the gloom
our pockets full of pearls. Given hunger, given cold,
what could we be to our new Ma, more than two
ill-fitting shoes, more than smudged, unswaddled need?
Should we have worked to charm her then, to weave
strands from our flaxen heads into her coarse plaits,
massage her hands with tears and anise seeds? Could she
have ever come to love, even the homegrown kind,
born from doing for? And didn't we deserve
the doing for?
> *But in her way, perhaps she cut*
> *to motherhood's first care—to endure,*
> *to hone that sharp survival, fingernails to the board,*
> *teeth to the clean, white bone.*

NOSE TIP,

you're barely a fused rib,
just an elbow-bend,

beginning. Dark seeds
dream into two eyes,

you are sealed in,
new-limning. Kindred

kidney-hulls conjoining,
lungs on the verge

of dawning. A heart's
first gravity-testing.

Mass of moss-bone
hardening, you unfurl

in fiddlehead digits,
you string coral

to line a spine-strand,
your moon-skull

floats tall on the tides
it calls. Ink whorls

on each thin heel-skin.
You weave strands

of tender tendons, vein
nets across your ocean.

Small world, new formed
bright surface, fresh carved

by our fingerprints
yet unmarred.

WHEAT FIELD WITH CROWS

after Van Gogh

The crows swim
in dense brushstrokes of sky.

Waves flatten them
to dark facsimiles of waves.

They rest on, are pressed on, arcs
whose shapes their bodies take.

Their metal cools in a mold
that will not crack.

Below them, wheat breaks
toward a different shore. It sways,

snakes upward, but is held down.
The thickness persists.

A path creeps deep
into the wheat, then drowns.

TIDE POOLS

I.

Temperatures near tropical
in winter shallows
warmer than typical

full-fledged sea, this
just-unlidded starscape stares
flutters, slows, as if, as if

it had nowhere to be or go
now that tide has flown, leaving
glittered shadowed armory:

starfish, clam, anemone
and this offense—four white
and knobby feet, outsiders

treading in this home,
ginger near fragility.

II.

My first time out,
he walked me
to the very edge
then told me:
watch your step.
He did not hold my hand.
It was not all
like that.

Later we leafed
through texts
of illustrated tragedy:
a stingray's sword
through foot or calf,
a face inflamed
by jellyfish.

We sat and watched
the tide recede,
inscribing on the shore
with each return
a slightly shifted story.

III.

The shore sings to her sea: *Why do you roam?*

The sea sings back: *I'm looking for my marriage bed.*

The shore: *Come lie with me. I'll build a bar to cradle you.*

The sea: *You can't hold all of me.*

IV.

Not our home. Museum of living things. Full of the force that touches
all. The sea, the breathing sea. Take me somewhere I can be. The sea, the
breathing sea.

V.

Here I am a reef, a shelf, here I am an anchored thing,
a paradise for barnacles, a long-forgotten submarine.
Ray and eel and angel fish all make their home in me.

My spine zippers against the sand, the brine braises my face.
I see the world through muddled eyes, I blink against
the salted lash. I adapt to hardly breathing.

The rock I brought is on my chest, I'll link
my feet through iron hooks. I'm staying,
I'm sustaining, a bulwark, no, a captive.

VI.

We want to get
to the bottom of it.
We want to see through it.

VII.

Maybe the pool is a mirror, a home,
a love note to the sky.

Maybe the pool is a drowning hole,
an unfillable mouth
an unblinking eye.

DEAR DAUGHTER,

dear dove, dear dream-
never-was,   dear stronghold, dear strangled, support

dear wall   between his ire and me, dear cherished
charitable sort   dear maker-up and maker-better

dear duster, fixer, arranger   dear wit-
before-strangers, siren at danger

dear crutch, dear ladder, dear door   dear green
grasping reed bowed back in the storm   dear grace

dear charm, dear means to disarm   dear child
dear kind, dear kin   dear kindling willing

to cradle the log   ignite
        would you, dear, the hearth's done flame

SWEET SEED, SWEET POISON

Sweet seed, sweet poison, sweet possibility,
how hard you harbor ships in me, how fast
you auger holes in sides and latch with fingers
on. Sweet present, portent, sweet pasture
welcoming cows to fold and field,
the gate cocked wide and bold, a damning
of the fences. There's no permission,
permitting here, just clear cut
thrash and burn and catch
as catching can, and catching all.

TO THE ARTIST'S CHILD

Sweet unwanted one:
seek out a new address.
Like the squirrel cared for
by cats, the deer nursed
by a dog, find a corner
in a nest of a kindly
mother hen, one who knows
no other love or job. Go
before this woman turns her head,
before ambition starts to snarl
and pull. Go before the house
grows hot with urge,
with inspiration. Go before
her silence sheathes
instead of sloughs,
before she shuts herself
into her room, pregnant with new
creation: the kind that will
sit still and never utter,
the kind that brings deep
feeling but not trouble,
the kind she can, if she's
not satisfied, start over.

PRE-TERM

And if he comes in the seventh month
before the thirty-second week. And if he looks
more newt than squirrel, lids still fused
and head enlarged, pink hands
just shy of webbing. And if his skin
hangs off his bones, still wanting fat.
And if those bones are cheese, not stone,
more air than marrow. And if his lungs
are zippered shut, alveoli suction cups.
And if his little body, lighter than a new potato
vined in tubes and cords, a heated lamp
to keep it warm, is borne away to another room
for close revision, and you still chained to your own
blank bed, then, then, will you still wish
you'd defied their orders: risen, written?

CHILD'S STORY

I'll tell you a story, Mama.
A boy goes on a journey, Mama.
His mama says, "No journeys."

Already my son understands how to birth a story, the push-pull of people with different wants, threat in the shape of one who disobeys. He crafts suspense: the heart-spark of the child on the verge of flight, the heart-stop of the mother of the flying child.

Then he goes to the forest.
Is that the scary part?

He tests my face. He knows there must be a scary part, knows the unknown is where fear resides, that lurking in the leafy green may be something enticing, erasing.

He meets a lion.
Is that the scary part?

No matter no lion lives near this state, no matter the name of the threat, the metaphor poised to break my tender boy.

And the lion is hungry, Mama,
and the lion attacks him.

I keep my face, my voice quiet. I am not sure the child is dead; I wait for what hero or moral will pop from this darkness.

And then his mom comes looking for him.
And she meets the lion.
And she says to the lion, "Please eat me."

I ask why she wants the lion to eat her.

She wants to see the boy again, Mama.

And he knows just what I would do, just what I would say, that I would scour the lion's stomach for my son, that I would join my son in the interior, that I would not go on without my son, that I would tear the lion throat to haunch as it opened its jaws to receive me.

And the lion eats her.

Then she finds the boy.

In what condition, I want to ask, but don't, waiting for him to explain if the two are stewing in lionly innards or the two are holding hands, Jonah-and-the-whale style, ready to tickle the lion into launching them toward safety.

And no such ending comes, just the mystery of why my son circles around eaten children, searching mothers, and the need to create something that scares me, gets a rise, a reaction, reassurance perhaps that I would be that mother, diving into the unknown, ready to fill her hands with whatever she could salvage.

BECAUSE WE LEFT THE CITY

Because we left the city, we left the rain behind
because we left the city, we left the mud behind
the loam and shale and gravel layers—
because we woke amazed that oaks
could grow so bold in silence, as if they fed
on secrets, because we walked one night
through heat still rising, released from where
it seeped and steeped through afternoon
because the sidewalks welcomed us
with root-shot faces, voices clawing
bug-bit ankles, because the cracking
earth in our backyard bore dirt-caked toys
enough to choke a lost child's room
bones enough to fill up his lost dog
because the sky would break each day
and pour and flood the haunted homes
and we'd endure, because it wept
upon our floor, our shoes, because we slept
unsure what rain would next exhume
because we left the city, we left the rain behind.

UNITS OF MEASURE

That year admission to a movie was two
burritos, the cost of a house on my street
three IPOs. In the time it took
to walk from Fourth and Mission
to Twenty-Second and Dolores
playing and replaying what went wrong
I could have composed a song,
figured out a new way to bake
an eggless cake. San Francisco is one-third
a marathon, small enough to walk across,
small enough to find you on a corner
in the Lower Haight wearing a green sweater
under green eyes, which were enough.
Then, nights were minutes
and days were weeks and weeks were waiting
to see who the next President would be.
The news was you threatening to move to Canada
or Italy, the sitcoms were me believing it.
My birthday was two hemispheres,
summer for you in Peru, winter for me
at a funeral in Virginia; our reunion was
one urinary tract infection, eight hours on the phone
with friends discussing what had changed,
one step closer to therapy. You measured affection
for me in "for now"; I for you in strength
of stomach clench, the food
I couldn't eat. The homeless man
we passed en route to that last movie
mistook hands held, proximity
of bodies for forever, warned us
not to let it go; you gave him
one weak smile not equivalent
to bread or money.

AUBADE

I wake and your face is a stranger's.
I wait for fear or lust to whisper which kind.
A dream crosses your lids
and you mumble an answer.
Familiar now: stubbled cheek, slow smile.
In your sleep you ravel around me, hungry
nestling your nose in my folds.
Is this what makes a family:
the way we shelter against
the darkening city
the way our blood-thinned limbs
tangle in winter. Your head turns slightly
to a sound beyond the window
and your arms tighten their hold.
Each night we close our doors
and trust each other. I knew
I knew you when you'd change and not
unmend me.
Never before have I felt
such absence of cold.

ABANDON

Let us not ignore the father
his back's reflection in the mirror
as he shuffles past the front door's
frame, noses to whatever harbor
he selects. Let us not accept
his provisions as "providing for"
that a moth-bit bag of coin and bread
and even sweat will keep a larder fresh
or forge sufficient warmth in winter.
Let us not permit his hidden shutters
to draw and lock, the lids inside
his eyes to drop and curtain.
Let us not declare the world of men
a sacred one, enclosed so women
cannot tread or brush aside the webs,
collect and brew the nettles, upend
the heaving, breathing box of hornets there.

PROPOSAL

In a field he asked.
I answered.

A fawn's ears rose above the way
as witness.

From afar we'd seen this
ambulant orange

—could be a fox,
could be a fire—

We approached
and it appeared: a deer

gangly-kneed,
all spots and sheen.

Oh, Love—
Tonight the dust

will twist
a falling beam

of light into a sunset.
What can we know

clearly,
from this distance?

THE BIRTH OF DOUBT
for CT

When he comes he is Tom, he is Thomas, the doubtful, the doubter, when he arrives he cries wide and full-fearful, uncertain, alive. Always he's Thomas, his conception's dim vision, the should-we or shouldn't- and later, much later, you will name him a teenage mistake made by two married folks. When you first feel him cluster, when he's just a cell-huddle, just a tadpole just a chicken-eyed mumble, he is Tom, he is Thomas, the doubtful, the doubter, and will you or won't you allow him to grow? You're listening close, you know the world doesn't love, no, the world doesn't love, when a woman says no. And later, much later, he makes space in your hull and you wonder, will you claim him, will you name him your own? Will he pass from these arms, to the arms that pass on, to the arms that pass over, to a world that won't love a woman who won't love her own? He is Tom, he is Thomas, in your laboring labor he is rowing through tides, he is backing and forthing, the doctor says three to six days of these false contractions, but he will take eight, a week and a day, of rapping his still-forming skull on the door of your womb. He is asking for shelter, he has heard the heart whisper that love is no surety, though he can be sure he is Tom, he is Thomas, he is yours, yours the doubter, the doubtful, the mother who called him to live in this still-shift- ing world, this uncertain home.

ADVICE TO MY YOUNGER SELF: FALL

This is no father, man of sticks and splinters.
A kindling heart, unaware that each match will catch
its passions. Remember, it's never enough to banish

flint from the kingdom. A field mouse will reveal
the alternate route to the hideout, the spinning-
wheel's spindle always arrives on the crone's cart.

And this is no mother, woman of bread crust
and broom dust. Consumed in mapping her shadow,
turns her back while dogs and rats roam the larder.

It's not that your songs don't amuse. It's not
that the tricks of your little bird hands do not please
or that you should search harder, run faster

from forest to field to hearth with your harvest
of seeds, extra mouthfuls for all, in your pockets. No.
If the pond swill ever stills to a glass fit for scrying,

here's what it might show: In the hollow tree's hull,
blind, furless kits hiss, as the falcon describes its circles.
But in the room with no door, no one ever knocks or enters.

RAVELING ROUND THE LAKE

Raveling round the lake the path,
the pointlessness. A thought
refrained from blooming.

If a circle is a wish
I'm weary now with wishing,
the walkers on this shore

waste more than just a Sunday.
The light will take its long low bow
round afternoon, the geese will fill

with swimming, they'll fall
to preening in what trickles down
around among them:

a white so cold with wanting.
When ever did we give
up endings, trade them in

for middling, a muddling lean
and lingering? Tonight's more apricots
and longing, a yellow so red

an orange inflamed
with warming, oh, to swallow
all that waning sun.

DUST STORM

This is what I know
of the man refusing burial:

A child, he crawled home from school
through a hurricane of dust.

Oklahoma landscape so abused
no crop held it in place.

I don't know if the story's true, but
I'm telling it. His eyes sealed

against the lash. Ears encrusted
with fine grains. A howling unrelenting.

A life inside the words "to scour."
To breathe, to swallow that glassy earth.

WE CANNOT SLEEP ALONE

Between three and four we're lovers, four to five warriors, you
feast and linger at my breast, then reject me bodily. This latching
on then pulling back, gums clenched to nipple taffy. My body
made to feed and yours consume and gnash, dispense with me.
My son, my love, my tiny enemy.

VERGE

Spring-formed, honed, run-ready,
I was a switch, almost thrown,
I was a pulse, quickening.
I asked the wind, what do you know,
I asked the wind to warn me.
My shuttered eyes grew sensitive
to figures framed in doorways.
I slept with one ear always up,
attuned to nighttime's yawn and creep.
I slept with shoes upon my feet.
I learned to dream of getaway
so even if but half awake, I'd move
and move precisely. I kept the burner on.
I was coiled, I was quivered, I was cocked.
I was a sudden summer storm
gathering, ready to rage then blow
myself to droplets: diffuse, ungraspable.

CHILD,

you cry real tears in the kitchen crib as I write in the bedroom. At one
end of our home your father plays a steady bass and counterpoint,
clocked by metronome, and you can hear him—as can we all—
and wonder why he does not rush to tend your howling. You don't ask much.
In fact, you're nearly powerless, except to use your voice's different tones:
want and need and urgency, the steady rise—
                                        And with each fall
I hope you've given up on us, trust that in the morning we will wake
right at your side, bright and nurturing, but night, night-
time's when we hide and fill our hands with all the day does not allow:
a pen, a page, piano keys, or selfishness, its low and keening call.

EPITHALAMIUM ON A THEORY OF GRAVITY

for David and Lorena

The apple will fall to the Earth.

You may wake
to the cry of a child
in the night,
testing gravity, the pull
of one creature on another.

You may wake
to find your body
expanding, a solar system—
organs, ventricles, ribosomes,
intercostal constellations
orbit a bright, beating sun.

In the beginning,
heavy elements released by stars
became the planets,
became the body.

In the beginning,
the adjective *gravis* meant heavy.
And *gravitas:* seriousness, dignity.

You may wake
to the heat of fusion,
your face toward the face
of a luminous other, two bodies,
inextricable binaries.

The Earth will fall to the apple.

Look out the window—
it's not the moon
pulling the tide
of this sea change.
It's not the moon
filling the room with light.

THE BARNYARD OF IT

on a line by Carmen Giménez Smith

The barnyard of it.
The restless pig at teat of it.
The blind and grubbing
mammal, rooting, smacking,
screaming when it won't flow fast
enough, the factory, the food groups
I've become. The small and swaddled
squirminess, the hunger pangs widening
to press out piss, the belly punch of gas,
the skin shellacked with milk, the eye lids flaked
by mucus rocks that will not drain through still-plugged
ducts of it. The pressed-against-me-constantly, the shifting
wrestling weight of it. The rock pushed up a hill of it.
The gravity, the equal, ever more opposing force of it. The ox-cart's load,
the furrowing plough, the seed scatter and prayer for rain of it.
The pecking orbit of a scavenger, extracting ore, oblivious
to the scarecrow's stare, the troubled trough,
the tantrumed vessel I pour
all my perfect in.

CREATOR, I TRY

To forgive my lack of art.
To forgive the dark hole
in the shape of a heart.
Humble now, tumble now,
crumble now, heart.
Only made of paste
and twigs, only a display
piece for empty eggs.
Robin-blue, pretty little
fragile thing, call your paper-birds
here to paper-sing.

ADVICE TO MY YOUNGER SELF: WINTER

One night you will learn you are soon
to be abandoned, cast outdoors.

This news may cause you some alarm.
Swallow it and savor those last hours.

You'll have years to assign the anger, blame.
For now hold them close. They'll keep you warm.

The day will start with a long hike. You'll receive
a crust of bread, an afternoon's low fire,

and you will take a nap, a few hours to believe
you are still loved, and maybe you misheard—

But night falls, and it's certain. You're forgotten,
left to freeze, starve, be eaten alive by wolves.

Allow yourself a moment's grief for all that's gone:
your cat, your clothing, your warm bed.

You may shed some tears,
but don't cry loud or long.

The cold will come; you'll need energy.
It helps to have a plan before you leave.

On your voyage out you can collect,
then drop along the road

the smoothest stones, the ones that reflect
moonlight, make a lighted trail home.

Or, as the story goes, you could crumble
up your crust of bread and leave a map

sure to be consumed by birds.
It hardly matters. Either way

you're lost. Either way
you'll wander into deeper woods.

DEAR CREATION, I CONFESS,

That I am the envy of others, that I know I am blessed. That I am blessed and yet I am plodding. That in the face of blessings I am resentful. That I feel rejected, though I give and give. That I have no more to give. That I demand my body have more to give. That I am asking for, waiting for, begging for more. That I do not know how to care for myself. That I know berating my body will not better it, will not urge it on, and yet I berate in an effort to urge on. More stick than carrot, more discipline, more punish. That I am impatient. That I hope and fear in equal measures. That I was made for this and yet I am not adequate. That I am less than others, that I am dry. That I have only this one last chance and I am too tired to try.

II.

FURTHER THOUGHTS ON ABANDON

I ache for it sometimes, H, you and I,
a table laid with nuts and fruits and meats,
more sweets than our wildest candy-store
imaginings, already wide-eyed at our fortune,
stumbling upon that home, an oasis of honey comb:
panes and shingles made of sugar, mint-stick
railings, gumdrop fences greeting us like miracles
after two days lost in snow-dense woods.
                              Wasn't it like falling
in love then? The steady pressure stilling
yawning walls of both our bellies,
gravies, juices, jellies seeping round
our tongues, the stains of foodstuffs
on our hands, fullness gathering
to usher us, distracted, past her dull-
red eyes, her rotten breath, her flesh
like a thing fresh-exhumed.
              Later, she would shut you in a stable,
fatten you like veal. Later, she'd fill a pot
in which we both could boil. And only after
I played ingénue then murderess
would all come right.
                              But let's ease back
into that night, an hour into dinner
after all our basic needs were met,
when I reached for seconds, you for thirds,
the fire lapping at our wine-flushed,
sweet-stung cheeks. Have you ever let yourself
feel that way again, dear H, listening wholly
to your pleasure, ignoring all else,
heeding the body's needy reason first?

TWO = PART INVENTION

Tender, sometimes, I feel
breath-took by the perfect
line of your spine. Your sturdy
calves lengthening, feet still
turning inward when you
stumble-run, but eyes full
of some kind of frolic
to keep you bobbing, aloft,
in laughter often, testing
notes against air.

PERFECT WIFE

Be doing be done.
Be done unto be under be asunder
but holding strong. Be slow thighs be
patient eyes be looking blindly at.
Be a pretty putty tat. Be blank be long
be sleek and strong enough for a woman
but made for a man be made for baking and tea
be pies cooling in the shade of sills and eaves.
Be leaves leaflessly falling be someone's true
calling be melon balling and drawling be celebratory
emotive syllabics fantabulatics dramatics and static cling
be anything that makes them sing. Be merry be bright
be pearly froth and silky tights be flashbulbs popping
on the stockings' glitterseam, be cream be dream, dream, dream.

PROCESSIONAL

He's asleep again
in afternoon
leaving all the world
to tend. I did
not know I'd wed
a glacier till
chill crept
through our room,
till roar of rock
like teeth against
enameled teeth
fractured my sleep.
I cannot track
his movement
with my eyes.
I yearn to run
across his glassy
back, to shake
his anchored shelf.
More frozen even
than my will.
He's teaching me
to let things happen
in their time.
Let progress progress
slowly. I'll drop my
sharp-edged thoughts
beneath our bed
tonight. Tomorrow
polish stone.

HOW I LEARNED TO LOVE

I.

One morning you learn
that when a man says,

If I hurt you again,
I'll kill myself

it does not mean you are safe.

II.

Like every story: a hero, a villain.

Home in Dust Bowl poverty.
College at fourteen.
Doctor, father, founder of
the Nation's First Eye Bank: Old Dominion.
Protected, defended, reputed, remained.
Manners, humor, social grace.

When his wife has him arrested,
committed,
the heads of family declare her dead.

III.

He may lift a glass and drink.
He may walk out a door.

He may drown himself
in an affair.

He may self-medicate
with morphine.

He may fly his own plane
fast into the ground.

There is more than one way
to leave a family.

IV.

My mother says I did my best
to marry a man who was not my father,
only to marry the father I'd never seen.

V.

I wake into my lover's face,
each pore and scar and lash.

OFFERING

Dear wolf, dear ravenous, dear raven,
who will peck and click at these remains?
I have saved for you this white leg, I have saved
you from the watchman's beam, the hunter's
muzzle. I have cordoned a corner, salvaged sanctuary.
For you I roll, for you I puppy-prance,
bared belly, dignity discarded, spread myself
like jelly, jam, sweet-cheeked, a mint-crisped
Easter lamb.

CROSSROADS

Bonnet cocked, ears flopped,
under a wig prop he said,
what matters is truth

fur muzzle, tooth dazzle,
scent of blood and vermouth
the truth about people

flat iris sparkle under
hungry eye gargle
people you love.

WE WANTED MORE

We wanted our old thoughts in our old heads,
our old music in our ears.
We wanted silence.

We wanted clarity, to see
no impish faces facing our own, breathing in
our out-breaths

no sticky fingers twining through our hair, our clothes,
our own now-sticky fingers. We wanted no swift foot
in gut or groin, no small fists against our cheekbones

while we slept,
no sucked-on thumb thumbed in our eyes, surprise,
we wanted acreage, our own bed for rolling in, sheets

we did not have to share, we wanted time to do the things we loved
and even things we didn't love but felt we had to do. We wanted you—
away—we wanted only us—

a moment of what used to be before you both appeared, those giddy
awful days of doubts about each other—
Now look at us, too occupied to bother.

LATER

August's edge
and the slimmest
glimmer of wither.

Foxglove fades
and bees harbor
like ships in slips.

You grow faster
than grass drunk
on sun and misting.

Thumb and pointer
precise, pluck tiny pine
needles, bother blades

of gladiola soon
to tower over crowds
of weeds. Already

I am missing
your fingers' first
unfolding, your

thin iris's
green-blue
bloom.

SOMETIMES, SILENCE

I knew to be
      hush, hush, hush
  I knew to seek
        quiet, quiet, quiet

  I knew not to ruffle
        untidy or enter
  I knew not to hum
        murmur or tremble
  I knew how to slip
        slant and dissemble

I kept
      hush, hush, hush
  I wept
        quiet, quiet, quiet

IN WHICH I FIRST DISCOVERED

Quite suddenly, at least it seems in retrospect
Though I still seek a complete

My relationship to my past
It was as if my past had taken

Without warning, understand,
Had slipped in such a way that it uncovered

No, that's not right for it suggests a lack of deliberate
It wasn't that I didn't try

And I don't mean that there were crimes but
How can I

Rather, without ceasing to mean, my memories
They were to be handled and observed without

As if they
Or maybe they

I discerned the possibility of the hidden
And I set out to find

It didn't
It wasn't

Should I have been ashamed
And it may have been too late

So I gathered what I knew
Not the truth, exactly, more of

That was the feeling. And on the strength of it
I undertook to write.

ENCOUNTER

I'm calling because I met Mr. Kitty in a parking lot
and he gave me your number.

I'm calling because it's Houston and humid and a Tuesday
and he looks like he hasn't bathed.

A healthy cat bathes.

I'm calling because I have trouble not feeling responsible,
and you have trouble keeping your cat inside.

Not that I don't know it's hard sometimes. Keeping it inside.

I wouldn't have called if it didn't feel urgent.

I wouldn't have called if it didn't merit
our talk, two strangers, two people getting on just fine
before this, before now.

You were just fine, weren't you?

I'm calling because it's three days till my birthday
and my doctor says I should be in pain.

I wasn't in pain.

Do you have anything for pain?

I'm calling because I remember only two moments in life
I've lived without fear.
Both were in dreams.

I'm calling because something this morning made you
leave the door open.

I'm calling because we live among forces beyond our control.

I'm calling because I don't know if what I do anymore
is kindness or desire.

Do you have anything for desire?

SPIDER SEASON

August and a spider season.
Wolf and hobo spiders thread
their way across our threshold,
repairing each day's damage
with diligence, what we destroy,
casually, while opening a door,
climbing a stair, what we destroy
purposefully, with a hand,
a hose, a broom. They'd bind us
if we let them, forcing
and reinforcing their mummy-wrap,
their swaddling strands, their sticky ribbon.
I've mixed feelings about razing
another's home; I've always admired spiders,
their artistry, sufficiency.
When I find them inside, I scoop
them in cups, scare them onto fliers,
grab a strand of silk as it pulses
from the belly, usher them outdoors,
as if to say, one space is mine,
one space is yours, and yet we co-occupy
and overlap, the boundary unclear. I loved
a man once, with arachnophobia
so deep, to merely hint
that one lightly tufted leg had nicked
his arm or neck was to meet
a quivering wreck of a man.
He could not survive here, where
the ceiling's a playground, junctions
between walls inspire commuters
to traverse on silken highways,
and even the bathtub with its hard-

to-grip sides, hosts the lone spider
hoping for a clumsy fly.
                              It's August
and I'm losing my hair, the effects
of nine month's estrogen increase
plus three postpartum months
of slow-released hormonal stores
until I'm menopausal at age thirty-
six; nature plays sneaky tricks
to keep her babies safe.
I am tired, worn down, uninspired,
and ill-equipped for much beyond
feeding this big belly with small lips.
His hands have just begun to grasp,
without intent, my hair, and I find it webbed
around his fingers, woven in his clothes.
To keep him quiet I secure
him in a swaddle sack, I plug
his mouth, a spider coddling her tender fly.
He wriggles free and sucks me dry.

MASTER

Your eyes, my love, are just dark spots that wish
to blink, your arms, your legs just buds that move
more like ideas than limbs that bend and haul, propel
you through the deepening pool. Your hands
don't clasp and yet you pull the string that clangs the bell
that sends me clambering. You don't know me yet but
know that I am yours, I've signed the line that certifies
I'll give it all and more. You draw my blood around you
like a sweater. You fill my veins with water. You push
your will onto my own and sit upon my bones
and bend them to a carriage fit for one.
You ride me home.

WANTING NOT WANTING

I wandered on the windy way.
I wanted nothing.

Extended my gaze toward a traveler
taking time, taking terrible, tangible

sweet-tooth time. I looked high
and low, I looked long. I forgot

the tune, the words, the song.
I stepped one foot two foot one foot.

I made a telescope of hollowed oak limbs
and lenses purchased from a peddler.

Oh Lord, the birds, they sang for my amusement.
Oh Lord, they scattered when I ran.

Shreds of tulle and gingham.
A boot unlaced. A mystery unnamable.

The trail a mass of ruts and mudguts.
The long winter's walk away from home.

PRESAGE

It is the phone ringing
in the night, a persistent call
of one bird across the lake

the prickling ear of the watchdog.
We do not articulate why we wake,
like horses sensing change in weather—

It is language we would not interpret,
everything forgotten, meant to be forgotten.
Lines to rewrite or ink over.

We would shut the bedroom door,
submerge ourselves in silence,
sew our eyelids so not to see.

But it tips toward us, this inevitable opening
spills onto our hands, our hearts. We are silk
and it runs, taking hold like dye.

HUSBAND,

husband me like a lost sheep,
shear me with your markings. Kneel
next to my hard bleating. Buff my hooves
with your bare hands, massage my knees
if they may wobble, warm my ears
inside your mouth. And when I'm well
and fat with wool, cast me not into the herd,
but hold me like I'm due for mending.
Fold me in your fleece-lined coat,
let me never wander from your tending.

ON A PHOTOGRAPH

He must have held the unsmiling face
of his ten years' wife, preserved

in black and white—a moment
of spring they'd stopped to record—

she, stern on the landmark's steps,
offset by dogwood blossoms.

He would have pressed the picture flat
upon a page of his new book,

now worn and cracking in my hands.
He later wrote with even strokes

above her face: *What are you thinking?*
As if to speak would have been

to want too much, as if a man
and woman might live silent

side by side, as if the question
wasn't meant for her, but me,

as if to say, *you see how she was,*
how I never knew, you see

a husband's care, his fear,
a stranger's resignation.

CARRYING ON

Look at how this day stains the next,
how a leak in the roof will rot
a beam in the attic, how water
runs a brown-bordered river down
the wall. How the smell permeates,
how we long to hang a sheet
or move a shelf, how we search for words
to cover it all, the accident of yesterday
speaking through today. This morning
I awoke, and half the bitter twilight
hung coat-like in my closet. *Come here*
said the dark, and wrapped me
in its long, barbed sleeves.

IT DID NOT HAPPEN AS YOU'D HOPED
for LB

If the Lear you flew into the earth
was not a bomb. If a crash

could not conceal careful choice.
If explosion did not act as cure

for your disease. If instead
it slipped under the soil like seeds.

If a tree rose from that burning ground.
If it bore a fruit we all would eat.

Then your death was not an end
to trouble but bloomed into a model.

UNSETTLING

While you slept the blackberries grew,
thistled beneath your inattention.

What did you leave on the table when you left
and why did you leave the table?

A neighbor says: *Way to not give up
on your lawn,* and you know her marriage is over.

Says she: *I trust him not
to get drunk while caring*

for the baby. She says: *I didn't miss him
when I swung.* Says: *I didn't miss much.*

LULLABY

Asleep with two shoed feet,
four small teeth above
four small teeth. Fingers
entwined in grandmother's
knit gift, breath falls, breath
lifts.

HUNGRY

I first deboned a chicken as a child.
Indifferent to the knife on flesh,
distant from the marbled eyes
that'd glistered in the roost.
But to snap a skeleton, to separate
a skull's rope-bridge from the fine
cervical spine, a shoulder-ball
from glove-like socket, to loosen the muscle's
weave, tear tendons that had married
fibers to each bone, to feel the force
that throbbed inside my slender thumbs,
well, it lit my rainless core.
And when I held the barn cat
on my lap or watched our ageing hound
half-sleeping at my feet, I'd speculate
what these hands might do.

Consider the pair who baked
a gingerbread son, the kind of kid
you'd rather taste than kiss,
or press your thumb into,
just to lick it afterwards, just
to leave a mark. I was not the first
to learn to love is to create
but also to consume.
Does the fire not stroke the woods?
The flood not wet the plains?

So when those two walked in that day
no more than children, though they wore
jawlines hard with wariness,
I knew my love could soften them,

could make them tender pets,
I knew my love was kindling-dry,
I knew my love would catch.

LITTLE SONG

Licorice, sweet gum, darkly hooded plum
flesh and pith kiss quick-fish tongue.
Pearl in strung sky, purrs a purple plosive
sigh, hiccups skip him nimbly off my sides.
Rib-walker from mung bean sprung,
swelling seasons under sun, from tadpolite
to parasite to night-light giving hum.
Impala wink on fox feet, rattle box and rain,
rigmarole, gravity pull, quintessential little
universe, this shotgun riding hitchhiker
on swiftly shifting tilting lifting track
for blooming trains. Oh leggy lamb of lamp-
glow, soon you'll swallow turquoise whole,
soon you'll drink my eyes my voice,
soon you'll wind your spring-run clock.
Tonight I herd your shadows in my flock.

CLUTCH

I hold this hurt to not forget the hurting.
I stretch it thin, a see-through scrim,
wet sheet on skin, a synapse-like-live-wire-
pulse with which to shock and stimulate.
I roll it wide, a canyon or an ocean.
I practice shouting over to be heard.
I hold it high because if dropped
it slinks and snaps my ankles, it sneaks in
or sneaks away. I hold it like a beacon
or a baby, a thing that leads me home,
a thing that needs protecting. This hurt's a wall,
granite uncracked by quakes, this hurt's a hole,
a wishing well, returning offers ten-fold, unfolded.

> *I used to cast my hurt along the road;*
> *it always came home hungry, begging*
> *that I take its pulse and treat it well.*

> *I learned to plant my hurt, to till it with a hoe,*
> *to harvest hurt, buckets, pockets full*
> *to carry hurt close to my heart, to bite*
> *straight into hurt, to swallow hurting whole.*

BEFORE AND AFTER

In the days after we'd see photos from the days before and feel the love that was different from the current love, the gut-dropping-unescaping pull toward who he already used to be.

* * *

When he came I feared I'd not possess him fully and not possess him soon enough. I knew him, had known him, his outsides pressed up against my ins, our sides beside ourselves. Yet I had not held, had not traced the arcs that limned his limbs. There he was wrapped in his un-knowableness, a mystery in a blanket, there he was quiet and quivering as if he might dissolve in moments of not looking, moments of forgetting to look.

* * *

Eyes closed I know that I look like him on the inside, that the expression that faces myself is his and the way my interior folds around itself mirrors the way his exterior is unfolding.

* * *

There were sounds in the world. The cry of a loose railing as I jostled the stairs, the squall of a cabinet opening. Sounds I had heard before without knowing they were his voice.

* * *

Never again a time before.

AFTERLIFE

In a parking lot your voice calls me
through a stone. M. says he saw your eyes:
a woman selling wind chimes—
that pleading look—as he showed her the door.
Where do the dead go when the living don't believe?
M. says you've been absorbed in the universal hum,
or you're a note now in a song, perhaps
you've been reborn. I need a place
to forward all your mail. I need a number
programmed in my phone. I search
each sidewalk for a sign, messages
in leaf-strewn ground. I comb my hair
the same way just in case you're up there now
looking here for me, a thousand stories down.

HUSH

Let's just say I was asleep
and now I've risen.
I prefer that we don't call it death,
but it's true, my life anchored
to a sunken ship, a woman bound
to a drowning man—is hardly living.

As for how I cut that rope,
let's just say I used a trick.
As for what they call me now,
let's just say it is not wife, help-
meet, or blessed-among-women.

It's true that women do conform.
When poured into a vessel
occupied by mystery, I was control.
With misery, I was contempt.

And now that I'm the keeper
of the cup I live in,
and now my cup is empty?

Let's just say I am both squall
and harbor, blaze
and air-tight room.

Let's just say that nothing
grazes in my sheets or greets me
by my hearth-side, that absence
is my perfect groom.

REVISION

Later, much later,
the smell of fur
and famine fades,
the heat of the scene
subsides. Later,
the air rises, escapes
each molecule present,
drifts, combines with other
better drafts, the scene
shifts subtly, not waiting
for witness, or understanding.

AMBITION

I scaled the rock face, goat-like, graceful,
    grateful I'd set aside time for scaling things,
        secured some stamina, the way in dreams
            you skim a surface, touching down
  at intervals, on the verge of flying, really,

only this was not a dream, more a riddle
    or a ladder, and I was moving up and up,
        each footfall was a hurdle. Each stair-step
            melted to a puddle once I passed, the mountain-
  side itself a mass of mud and ash, I made it up,

at last. I made it up. It was sunset, it was daybreak.
    It was a party on the peak replete with sacred
        texts. A wedding and a wake. Every thing
            becoming. The red sun bathed the snow-
  cloaked canyon near beyond and I'd just found

my camera. It was everyone I'd ever known
    and some who'd passed. I felt embarrassed
        it had been so long. I felt embarrassed
            by my letters of condolence; I should
  have known. Beyond the guests, time hung

like a scrim. Beyond the scrim another ridge,
    a family of false summits. So much to climb,
        so few breaths for climbing. Someone handed me
            a reckoning, a picture of the route I'd run.
  I looked up again and everyone was gone.

PREFACE

She's on the stairs and listening.
She's hastening. She's pulling strings,
unraveling. She's made up the mind,
a lunar thing that has the where-
withal to call a tide, to bring tidings
of deep sea change. You may wake
to the tap-tap of her finger,
a wave against your hull. You may stow
yourself neatly in a sealed room, but
you won't escape her call.
Pouting, now, she's powering,
she's a pounded ring, she's ore, she's filling
up its empty core. She's wanting more.
She's a figured thing, pre-figuring
your careful plans, she's rewriting
your almanac, she's standing at the ship's
big wheel, it's turning now,
she's sailing for your shore.

NEVER HAVE

Never have another wrapped
        completely in me never
                another bundle turn and tumble
never another stretch till you roll right over
        pull your sleeves into a slippy
fish-mouth four fresh teeth
        bloomed buds bared for tasting
            this whole world
                      Never that twitch
      as you drift sleeping whole form fit
to mine your hair my lips your cheek my breast
        your feet in the crook of the hook of my
life Never again so pressed to me
          never so perfectly blessed never
                these small pants socks like hats
      for my big toe never this untouched
        skin never cell's first division
        to millions
                of maps of perfectly
            you
        Never this blinding
          again new

CODA

In the strawberry bed
the leaves of the weeds
flare and fringe
just like strawberry leaves.

The mother who
watches you cry
as she eats a sandwich,
pays a bill, or sits
straight staring
at the windowsill

looks just like the mother
who starts in the night
uncertain of where
or why, only knowing
she must fly
toward your tending.

She does what she needs
to survive.

NOTES

Epigraph from Project Gutenberg's e-text version of "Hansel and Gretel" in the *Grimms' Fairy Tales*, collected by the Brothers Grimm.

The title and first line of "The Barnyard of It" come from *Bring Down the Little Birds*, by Carmen Giménez Smith.

ACKNOWLEDGEMENTS

Grateful acknowledgment to the following journals in which some of these poems have appeared or are forthcoming, sometimes in earlier versions or under different titles:

The Bennington Review: "Ambition"
Borderlands: Texas Poetry Review: "Presage"
Calyx: "Each Day I Open the Door to Damage"
Crab Orchard Review: "Advice to My Younger Self: Fall," "Advice to My Younger Self: Winter," and "Further Thoughts on Abandon"
Diagram: "The Flood"
inter/rupture: "The Barnyard of It"
Jack Straw Writers Anthology: "Child," and "Never Have"
The Laurel Review: "Wheat Field With Crows"
Many Mountains Moving: "Epithalamium on a Theory of Gravity"
The New Hampshire Review: "Units of Measure"
New Ohio Review: "In Which I First Discovered"
Nimrod: "Carrying On"
Ocho: "Encounter"
Pebble Lake Review: "Because We Left the City"
Poetry Quarterly: "Unsettling"
Squaw Valley Review Poetry Anthology 2010: "Lullaby"
Tule Review: "Hush" and "Raveling Round the Lake"
Watershed Review: "Little Song" and "Nose Tip,"
Zone 3: "It Did Not Happen as You'd Hoped" and "Proposal"

"Further Thoughts on Abandon" also appeared in *Northwind Poets Anthology 2010.*

"Advice to My Younger Self: Fall" also appeared in *The Far Field,* a blog curated by Kathleen Flenniken, the 2012–2014 Washington State Poet Laureate.

Gratitude to the following organizations that have supported my work and my development as a writer: Phillips Exeter Academy, Stanford University, Stanford Continuing Studies, University of Houston, Inprint, Lakeside School, Bread Loaf Writers' Conference, Summer Literary Seminars, Community of Writers at Squaw Valley, Artist Trust, Jack Straw Writers Program, Lighthouse Writers Workshop, and Colorado Academy.

I am grateful to many people who have been readers, listeners, cheerleaders, and inspirations. My family: Margaret and Rodolfo Pérez, David Pérez and Lorena Vignolo-Heim, Ileana and John Street, Edward Pérez and Laura Villa. The Houston team: Nina McConigley, Jill Meyers, Amanda Nowlin-O'Banion, Mónica Parle, Sasha West, and Tiphanie Yanique. The Seattle writing group: Erik Christensen, Ramón Esquivel, John Newsom, the Jack Straw 2013 alums, and the unforgettable Kim-An Lieberman.

Thanks to my writing teachers through the years: Fran Solether and Rex McGuinn; David Biespiel, Eavan Boland, Nan Cohen, W. S. Di Piero, Sheila Donohue, and Christian Wiman; Mark Doty, Nick Flynn, Tony Hoagland, Rubén Martínez, Adam Zagajewski, and especially to Claudia Rankine. To Francisco Aragón, Miguel Guillén, Stevie Kallos, and others who have taken a chance on me.

Thanks also to Stephanie G'Schwind and her team at the Center for Literary Publishing for building a beautiful book and shepherding me through the process.

My awe and gratitude for Jenny Tran, who produced yet another beautiful piece of cover art.

Finally, to Wylan and Felix for the anxiety, delight, and absolute love they've birthed in me, and to Matt for all that and more.

This book is set in Eyechart & Sabon
by The Center for Literary Publishing
at Colorado State University.

Copyediting by Melissa Hohl.
Proofreading by CL Young.
Book design and typesetting by John McDonough.
Cover design by Kathleen Naughton.
Cover art by Jenny Tran.
Printing by BookMobile.